TEACHER'S BOOK 1

What do *you* think?

PICTURES FOR FREE ORAL EXPRESSION

Donn Byrne and Andrew Wright

LONGMAN

Longman
1724-1974

Longman Group Limited
London

*Associated companies, branches and
representatives throughout the world*

© Longman Group 1974

All rights reserved. No part of this
publication may be reproduced, stored in a
retrieval system, or transmitted in any form
or by any means, electronic, mechanical,
photocopying, recording, or otherwise
without the prior permission of the
Copyright owner.

First published 1974
Fourth impression 1976

ISBN 0 582 52270 6

Printed by Lowe & Brydone Printers Limited, England

Contents

	page
Introductory note	iv
How to use this book	v
The Lesson Notes	ix
Useful language	ix
Guidelines	x
Guided oral exercises	xiii
Discussion	xiv
Appendix 1 Organising group work	xvi
Appendix 2 Some grammatical features of colloquial English	xvii
Key to Symbols	xx
LESSON NOTES	1

Introductory note

The visual material in the accompanying *Students' Book* (the first in a series of two), has been compiled to provide practice in self-expression for learners of English as a foreign or second language.

The pictures are intended to be interpreted and discussed — rather than simply described — and then related to the student's own experience and background. They provide, therefore, talking-points around which different kinds of oral practice can be developed.

Detailed guidance in procedures is given in the following section **how to use this book**, and teachers are strongly urged to study this carefully before attempting to use this material in class. The rest of the *Teacher's Book* contains lesson notes on each picture and suggestions on how to play the games which appear in the latter part of the *Students' Book*.

This material may be used to supplement *any* main coursebook at levels ranging from elementary to advanced. In particular it will be found valuable for certain oral requirements of the *Cambridge Syndicate* examinations with effect from 1974.

How to use this book

Introduction

Most students *want* to talk. They also have *something* to say. This is shown by the way they burst into conversation in their mother tongue as soon as they leave the classroom. How can we harness to foreign language learning some of this desire and capacity to talk?

The old-style 'conversation lesson' was an attempt to give language learners practice in self-expression. It acknowledges their need and wish to communicate. But this type of lesson was rarely successful, and it is instructive to consider the reasons for this.

a *The size of the class*   Except in small and privileged classes, the individual students rarely got enough practice. Often the lesson tended to be monopolised by a few talkative students.

b *The teacher-class relationship*   The teacher's presence can be inhibiting. Is he really interested in *what* we have to say, the students wonder, or *how* we say it? To them the teacher must sometimes appear as a kind of watchdog, helping and correcting only with the language. Some students make mistakes or dry up altogether simply because they feel that the teacher is watching them (and the same thing happens when they have to talk in the presence of the whole class). But with only their peers present and especially within the intimacy of a small group where everyone knows each other, students relax, their personalities expand and talk begins to flow.

c *The arrangement of the classroom*   Except in small classes students cannot talk to one another. To ask a student to stand up when he speaks introduces yet another inhibiting factor. Consequently they tend to address the teacher rather than one another, while the remaining students 'listen' without facing the speaker, rarely involved in what he is saying. This makes it impossible to develop the free exchange of ideas.

d *The lack of an appropriate stimulus*   This may be viewed from two angles:

(i) The students need a stimulus to arouse their imagination and set their ideas flowing. A 'topic', coldly served up, will rarely do this.

v

Skilful teachers, of course, know how to stimulate their students, but it is hard work and often results in the teacher doing too much of the talking himself.

(ii) The students also need a stimulus which will generate practice within the limits of their language attainment, otherwise they make too many mistakes or simply fail to express themselves at all. This is a big problem, and will be reviewed later in the light of the recommendations below.

From this analysis, what kind of procedures should we use in the classroom and what kind of material do we need to stimulate self-expression?

The problems identified in a, b and c above may be largely resolved by reorganising the class. The class, after all, is a purely arbitrary unit whose size may vary. We may be tempted for various reasons (time, discipline etc) to teach all the students together at all stages of learning, but this would be misguided. At the *presentation* and *practice* stages of learning, when students are exposed to and learn to use for the first time new items of language, it is both effective and economical to teach the whole class as a single unit (although even at the practice stage it will be necessary to 'pair' students off so that they can work to some extent on their own and thus get the maximum amount of meaningful practice). But at the *production* or *communication* stage, when we are concerned with getting students to use the language for themselves, it becomes increasingly difficult to preserve the class as a single unit for the simple reason that it does not provide an environment within which the students can communicate.

The solution lies in dividing the class up into smaller units or groups. How these are organised is explained in detail in *Appendix 1*. Here it is sufficient to note that the group, made up of perhaps 6-8 students under the direction of a group *leader,* whose function is to co-ordinate the activities of the group and to serve when required as a link with the teacher, is a largely autonomous practice unit. The activity which the students are to undertake is defined by the teacher and discussed first with the whole class, but after this they are allowed to work by themselves. Divided into groups, the students are now able to sit together, facing one another in a small and intimate circle, rather like a club meeting, and talk freely. The teacher is still present, and he may even participate in the group activity, but he has abdicated his normal role and become something like a guide or consultant.

Of course it cannot be pretended that everything will go smoothly from the start (difficulties are also discussed in *Appendix 1*). Like all procedures (from chorus work, when the students have to work in unison, to paired practice, when they have to work on their own), group activities have to be learned and students have to get accustomed to them. But they quickly appreciate the value of self-directed activity, of being allowed to be 'agents in their own learning' and are encouraged by the results. Above all, they are motivated to *go on* learning because they become aware that they can use for themselves, on however limited a scale, the language they have learned.

We must also face the implications of group work, which we have recommended as providing the best environment for communication practice, with regard to the problem noted in **d** (ii) above. We have noted that the teacher will no longer be teaching the whole class nor will he even be supervising (except occasionally and then only in a discreet way) the activities of the groups. How then can he check or control what the students say? How can he be sure that they will not make mistakes? How can he correct mistakes if they make them?

The simple answer to these questions is that while group activities are in progress he cannot do any of these things, nor is it necessary that he should do so. At the *presentation* and *practice* stages, it is an important part of his job to see that the students are exposed to correct models of language which they learn to imitate and then produce under his guidance with reasonable accuracy. Here correction will be necessary. And while preparing the students for group work (at least in connection with the material in this book) the teacher will try to anticipate the language difficulties which the learners are likely to have and since they will be talking at this stage too he can make corrections then. But clearly he cannot predict all the language which the group activity will generate, and mistakes will therefore occur, as they occur in real-life situations. While we do not view this with complacency, we believe that at this stage the greatest mistake the student can make is not to speak at all and the greatest mistake the teacher can make is not to give him that opportunity. Besides it is not true that all mistakes will go uncorrected. Students are well able to correct one another. In the context of group work they are much more involved in what they are doing simply because they have been given the opportunity to assume responsibility for their activities. Consequently they listen with greater interest to one another and mistakes which would pass unnoticed in the course of class practice are quickly spotted by members of the group. The teacher too when he sits in on a group can listen out for mistakes and either correct them gently or, preferably, make a note to correct them later on a generalised basis. The students should always feel that when the teacher joins them he has come to listen to their ideas rather than check their language.

There is a further point to be kept in mind. Many students make mistakes when speaking a foreign language because they are too ambitious; they overreach themselves instead of staying within the limits of the language which they know. One important service which the teacher can perform is to demonstrate to the students through his own practice how they can stretch and exploit their stock of structures and words to express their ideas simply but effectively. This can be done especially at the time when he is introducing the group activity or winding it up, or at the discussion stage (see below).

It was pointed out in **d** (i) above that to get students talking they need to be given a stimulus which will arouse their imagination (a faculty which formal instruction tends to dull). Visual material is ideal for this purpose precisely because it is open-ended. We can interpret almost any picture, or series of pictures, in a variety of ways and at different language levels. The pictures in this book have been designed and selected with a view to presenting situations which will provoke both a variety of interpretation and discussion (in this respect some of course are more open than others). This immediately gives the students something *to talk about*. Take, for example picture 38 in the *Students' Book*. On one level this is simply a picture of a woman who is looking out of a window. This perhaps is how students are accustomed to looking at the illustrations in their textbooks: they contextualise the meaning of language items which occur in a dialogue or passage. They expect such pictures to have a clear and unambiguous meaning, and that indeed is their normal function. But what is 'given' in these pictures, the overt features, is less important, from the point of view of stimulating talk, than the 'unknown' elements which can be conjured up when the imagination is induced to operate (as it did when we looked at pictures as children). For example, referring again to picture 38, we do *not* know:

a   who the woman is;
b   what she has seen;
c   where the object (person or thing) is or where the event is taking place;
d   who she is talking to;
e   what she is saying.

Naturally every student will have his own ideas about these and will want to voice them: this is where self-expression begins. First, however, he will have to be shown how to look at the pictures from this angle so as to see their full potential and to appreciate that different interpretations are possible and all equally valid provided that they can be explained and developed. Eventually we may invite the students (either as a group or as a class) to agree on the best developed or most interesting or most amusing interpretation, but by that time a great deal of talk has been generated and the picture has served its purpose. We can now move on and relate the situation to the student's own experience. Do *you* do this? Have *you* ever seen anything exciting (or amusing or frightening) happening when you looked out of the window? In the experience of one of the authors using this material, a lesson that began with some rather pedestrian interpretation ended with the vivid account of a murder which one of the students had witnessed when he happened to look out of the window! It was perhaps an incident which he had never expected to have a chance to talk about in the language class.

The Lesson Notes

The lesson notes which accompany each picture are divided into four sections: Useful language; Guidelines; Guided oral exercises and Discussion. Each of these is now explained and illustrated with worked examples. It is not intended of course that all the activities proposed should be carried out within a single class period. It is left to the teacher to decide how long free oral expression should go on for and how often it should be introduced. Much depends on the level of the students. In the early stages 15-20 minutes might be an optimum length for practice (though one should never interrupt an activity which is going well) while at an advanced level it could continue for a whole period.

Useful language

Here we have tried to indicate, as the heading suggests, some of the patterns, phrases and vocabulary which are likely to be needed when the picture is being talked about. For the most part these refer to visible or implied features of the picture, for, as we have noted above, we cannot predict all the ideas which will be thrown up and consequently we cannot predict all the language that will be needed. However, in the course of discussion, students are likely to want to refer to some of these features. For example, for picture 3, the following patterns may be needed:

  a   help someone climb up on (*or* over) the wall
  b   climb on to someone's shoulders
  c   too high to climb over by oneself

In listing these patterns we are not suggesting that the teacher should formally teach them or write them up on the blackboard. The teacher should first of all relate them to the level of his class and decide whether his students know them (receptively or productively), whether they are all equally essential (for example, among those cited above, **b** is perhaps the most important) and whether they could not be expressed in a simpler way to suit the level of his students. For example, the idea expressed by **a** could be conveyed through two clauses: A cannot climb over the wall by himself, so B is helping him. It looks as if the phrase *by himself* will be needed, so the teacher should find some way of introducing it. The teacher's first task therefore is to *prepare himself* for talking about the pictures more or less *at the level of his students*. He might then introduce key phrases through a conversational exchange.

    T: Let's look at picture 3. Are you all looking at it? Now tell me something about the picture.
    S1: Well, there's a boy climbing up on the wall.
    T: Good. Or perhaps *over* the wall. Now, what's the other boy doing?
    S2: He's helping him.
    T: Quite right. Why?
    S3: Well, the wall's high.
    T: Exactly. It's very high, isn't it? So he can't climb over *by himself*. Do you understand that? He can't climb over by himself. How's he climbing up on the wall, then?
    S4: He's climbing up on the other boy's shoulders.
    T: Fine . . .

After this the teacher may repeat or invite other students to repeat key sentences, and some phrases, such as *by himself* and *on his shoulders*, can be written up on the blackboard. He might also have gone on, in the context of what has been said, to introduce patterns a or c.

This first stage is by no means essential. With advanced students it might be omitted altogether. Another approach would be to filter the language items into the next stage, when the students are being introduced to the discussion areas. In any case, it should be done rapidly.

Guidelines

Here the students are invited to begin to interpret the picture. This will normally be carried out in three phases. In the initial phase it will be necessary either to show the students from which angles the picture can be discussed or, once they have had some experience of working with this type of material, asking them to make suggestions themselves. This phase might run as follows:

    T: All right now. Let's look at the picture again. Now, who are these boys? Do we know?
    S1: No, we don't.
    T: Right. We don't know. We don't know who they are. Well, you can decide. Now go on.
    S2: Why is the boy climbing up on the wall?
    T: Quite right. We don't know that. *Why* the boy is climbing up on the wall. Why he wants to climb up on the wall. Have *you* any ideas? Good, but not now!
    S4: What is in the garden?
    T: Which garden?
    S4: On the other side of the wall.

T: But is it a garden? Perhaps it's a school! There's something on the other side of the wall, but we don't know *what*. Do *they* know? The boys, I mean.
S4: Of course they know! They ...
T: Well, wait! You can talk about that in your groups. Now can you talk about anything else?
S5: Yes. What is going to happen.
T: Good. We don't know that, do we? All right, you can talk about all these things. And perhaps there are others. Now let's go over them again. Who wants to tell us? ... That's fine. Now you can divide into your groups and talk about them.

As you can see, students often want to make up their minds too quickly; to decide on something obvious, like a garden (which may of course turn out to be quite satisfactory) before their imaginations have got to work. At this stage, while a warm-up along these lines is being carried out with the whole class, they should be gently discouraged from coming to any decisions. For this reason it is probably better to avoid asking direct questions because these encourage ready-made answers (and that is why the guidelines in the lesson notes have not been presented in question form). The important thing at this phase is to get them to think in general terms about the picture, to open their minds to its possibilities.

After this they divide into groups and begin to discuss the picture. The goal may be either to let them talk freely until they have nothing more to say, or to get them to arrive at a group interpretation. A discussion at this phase might go as follows:

S1: I think they're schoolboys.
S2: Yes, and they've just come out of school ...
S1: ... and they're going home.
S3: Yes, but who are they?
S4: Well, the boy on the wall is George.
S5: And the other one is John.
S4: They're friends.
S5: They're in the same class. They always go home together.
S2: But why are they climbing over the wall?
S1: Only George is climbing over the wall.
S2: Well, why is he climbing over the wall?
S3: There are some apple trees there.
S1: Yes, and they're hungry. They want to eat some apples.
S3: They're going to steal them.
S6: No, I don't agree.
S3: Why not?
S6: Well, I have a different idea. They were playing football.
S1: Well?
S4: What happened then?

S6: Well, George kicked the ball and it went over the wall.
S5: Yes, and they want to get it back.
S1: Whose ball was it?
S5: George's. So he's climbing over the wall.
S6: No, it was John's. But George kicked it, so he's climbing over the wall.
S3: Did he get it?
S2: Well, George was up on the wall and just then a policeman came along...
S1: He saw George and he said: 'What are you doing up there?'
S4: Yes, he thinks that George is going to steal some apples...

Eventually — though not as smoothly as this, of course, because there are many interruptions and arguments — the students assemble their interpretation. They may even fail to notice that there is some difficulty in an interpretation along these lines e.g. if George climbs into the garden, how would he get out again? A point like this is likely to be picked up in the class discussion which follows.

This is the third phase (not essential but usually quite interesting because the students are interested in what the other groups have been doing). When the class is re-formed, one or two students from each group have to act as spokesmen. Each can be asked to present their group's version in turn, after which the other students can comment and finally decide which is most interesting. If time is short, one group only can be selected to present its version, while the other students comment on it in the light of their own conclusions.

It must be acknowledged that under certain conditions or on certain occasions group work will not be possible. Obviously some discussion involving the whole class is possible, but with the limitations on practice which were noted at the start. Again if discussion starts in the course of the warm-up phase and promises to be lively, it should not be interrupted. An alternative procedure if regular group work is impossible is to form a special group which is given the job of talking about the picture while the remaining students listen critically. This in itself is good training, for they need to be taught to listen to one another with attention. To ensure their involvement the students can be given various goals (What was the most interesting suggestion? Who spoke the most? What mistakes were made?) and afterwards they should of course be given the opportunity to comment.

It is left to the discretion of the teacher to decide whether or how often students should be asked to prepare themselves beforehand for talking about a picture. This could be productive at all levels, provided that students are sometimes given opportunities for spontaneous talk. At an advanced level it could serve to deepen the discussion. There is always the danger, however, that students will be less flexible because they have become attached to *their* interpretation. In general they should be discouraged from preparing set pieces except when these are intended to provoke class or group discussion. For example, two or three students may be called on to give their interpretations, which are then compared and discussed. Alternatively, a single student may be asked to do this and is then exposed to questions and comments by the class. This kind of exercise helps develop listening with attention, which we regard as a valuable skill.

Guided oral exercises

Here two types of activity are suggested. The first is the production of dialogues (usually exercises i and ii). This should normally be done as group work and, if the teacher wishes, this activity can follow on directly from the oral practice discussed under *Guidelines,* while the students are still divided into groups. Usually the suggestions for dialogues relate quite closely to this. At least two groups should be assigned the same exercise, so that the results may be compared. First, then, the groups should develop their dialogues, which they will normally want to write down. They should then rehearse them and decide which two students are going to play the roles. When the class is re-formed, each group takes it in turn to act out its dialogue. These should not be long: usually four exchanges will be sufficient. A typical dialogue (Exercise ii) might run as follows:

Man: Hey! What are you doing up there?
George: Well, we've kicked our ball into your garden and I wanted to get it back.
Man: You wanted to steal my apples!
George: No, I didn't! Look, there's the ball.
Man: Where?
George: Near that tree. Can I have it?
Man: Oh, all right. Here you are. But next time don't climb over the wall. Come and ask me.

The second type of activity (usually iii, but sometimes two of this type are included) is a projection exercise. The student is asked to imagine himself in a situation similar or related to the one in the picture, and he is then set a communication task. For example (again with reference to the picture on page 3): *You have climbed into someone's (garden), and the person finds you there. Explain what you are doing there.*

Acceptable responses at different levels of linguistic attainment are given below.

a Please excuse me. I kicked my ball over the wall and I want to get it.

b Please excuse me. I kicked my ball over the wall and I climbed over to get it back. Look, there it is. Can I have it, please.

c Please let me explain! I'm not a thief, you know! We were playing football and I kicked my ball into your garden. So I climbed over to get it back. Look, there it is. Do you mind if I get it?

   d Look, you might give me a chance to explain. Anyone would think I was a thief! We were playing football in the road and I happened to kick the ball over the wall. So I just climbed over to get it back. Look, there it is, over there. By the tree. Do you mind letting me have it back?

This type of exercise is best done with individual students rather than as a group activity.

Discussion

Here we move beyond the picture and relate the situation to the student's own experience and, wherever possible, his environment. This can be an extremely rewarding activity but a word of caution is necessary. The questions listed are *merely suggestions*. It is not intended, unless the class is of a fairly high level, that the teacher should use these questions as they stand. First of all, he may decide that some questions are not suitable (on linguistic, personal and social grounds). Secondly, he should see if any of the questions need re-phrasing. For example, again with reference to the lesson notes on page 3, we have the question: *Would you be angry if the boy climbed into your (garden)?* This could be presented to the class in more simple language: *A boy has climbed into your garden. Are you angry?*

The questions in this section are divided into sets. Those in the first set tend to be personal, while those in the second set invite the student to reflect on his environment.*

Clearly this can result in some stimulating and challenging argument, especially in multi-national classes, and a class debate can be organised around some topics (this activity is developed in detail in Book 2). The second set of questions or a third one is sometimes presented in the form of a small project. For example, the students are directed to look at newspapers or magazines with a view to finding certain information, or are asked to find out about good restaurants or plan a holiday. With this type of activity language learning is fully integrated with their everyday life.

In these lesson notes it has been our intention to show how this visual material can be fully exploited. In so illustrating both the range and depth of these activities we are not advising teachers to try to squeeze the last drop of language practice out of every picture. Class interest is the determining factor. A picture can always be left and taken up again at a later date. In fact there is considerable advantage in this approach because the students can thereby appreciate how much more they can say about the picture. In this way it can serve as a kind of yardstick by which the students can measure their own language growth, and for the same reason can be used by the teacher for informal oral testing.

---

* In a few cases this type has not been included in Book 1

It is assumed that from time to time teachers will wish to tape-record some of these oral practice sessions. This will be especially valuable for the second and third stages.

Nothing has been said about written work and no suggestions are included in the lesson notes, since this is essentially an oral practice book. It is left to the teacher to decide which activities should be written up afterwards or which could be further explored through written assignments. Clearly, however, both the dialogue exercises and the topics for discussion could be treated in this way.

Finally, teachers are urged not to treat the visual material in this book as complete. On the contrary, both they and their students should supplement it as much as possible with pictures from newspapers and magazines, which can be then used to extend or deepen by comparison the range of discussion. These cut-outs can be mounted on card or kept in a loose-leaf folder. In particular, groups should be encouraged to build up their own collections, which can later be compared with or exchanged for those of other groups.

Games

Visual material which may be used for stimulating language games appears in the latter part of the Students' Book (pictures 57 to 69) and it is left to the teacher to decide when he should introduce them. They can often be used to provide a welcome break in the lesson but over and above this they offer a framework for oral practice which students find personally meaningful, because games are a natural form of self-expression.

The lesson notes on the games are in the form of a commentary showing how the games may be played in one or more ways. Teachers should work out beforehand what language items are likely to be needed by their class for the game which they have decided to play. Although new language items may be introduced in the course of a game, obviously the frustration of not being able to make the appropriate responses must be avoided. Some games are naturally suited to practising specific structures; others are more open-ended and for that reason best played at a more advanced level. Many games can of course be played at different levels.

The following points should be noted:
    a explain the game carefully beforehand, in the mother tongue if necessary;
    b give the students adequate rehearsal;
    c involve as many students as possible, dividing the students into either groups or teams as appropriate. When an element of competition is introduced, students generally play the game more enthusiastically.

Appendix 1

Organising group work

a *Structuring the group* The size of the groups has to be worked out in relation to the number of students in the class, but as a general rule there should be between five and eight students in each group and not more than five or six groups in the class. The groups should be formed by the teacher himself so as to include students of mixed abilities, on the principle that the students will help one another in different ways. Later on students may be allowed to change groups, and in any case re-formations may be necessary to prevent them from becoming gangs. Each group should have an identifying label (for mature students a number is quite sufficient), and a set position in the room to work in so that, when students are asked to do group work, they can begin with the minimum delay and fuss. Usually group work will involve some re-arrangement of the classroom furniture.

b *Group leader* Each group should have its own 'leader' ('co-ordinator' etc, whichever label is preferred). Initially he may have to be appointed by the teacher but, since he should be changed from time to time, the students may then be allowed to choose their own. The function of the group leader is not to dominate the group but to co-ordinate their activities and to serve as a link with the teacher.

c *The role of the teacher* The teacher's main task is to prepare the students (or sometimes the group leaders) for group work. Having done this, he should allow the students to get on with their work. However, he should encourage the students to consult him as the need arises and, depending on the activity and the level of the students, visit the groups and listen in. If he participates in an activity, he should try to do this as if he were a member of the group. Generally teachers will find that they are fully occupied while group work is in progress.

d *Duration and frequency* Many factors are involved here (the number of lessons per week, the level of the class etc) but once the students know enough language to use for communication activities - on however limited a scale - some group work should be carried out about once a week for about half a class period. Longer sessions may sometimes be needed (to complete a project, for example, in which the students are especially involved) and in general it is inadvisable to interrupt an activity which is going well.

e *Problems* Some teachers feel dissatisfied because group work is time-consuming and because they cannot see their students making obvious progress. It is true that progress cannot be measured as easily as at the practice stage, but it should be remembered that the students are not merely consolidating what they have learnt but using perhaps for the first time what they have merely learnt superficially at the earlier stages. This is of great motivational value and offsets the apparent disadvantage that group work is time-consuming. It is also sometimes argued that lazy students will take advantage of group work to be even lazier! However, since students usually get more deeply involved in group activities than in regular class work, laziness is unlikely to increase. Students may sometimes resort to the mother tongue. This cannot always be avoided and should be accepted if it is needed to further the activity in hand. The kind of activity envisaged in connection with this material will not normally require the use of the mother tongue and adequate preparation at the class level before group work begins will help smooth out linguistic difficulties. Finally, there may from time to time be problems of 'discipline'. We have noted that it takes time for the students - and the teacher - to get used to new procedures. Besides, the real problem is not 'active' indiscipline or bad behaviour, which can be easily spotted and put right (and in any case tends to disappear when students are involved in learning - even if this results in their becoming noisier) but 'passive' indiscipline in the form of non-participation, when students have opted out of learning. This, however, is much more likely to be present during class work than in group activities!

Appendix 2

Some grammatical features of colloquial English

The teacher is recommended to consult this checklist from time to time to ensure that his students are gradually building up a mastery of these items, for the most part receptively at the start (the teacher should use them freely when he talks to the class) and then productively. Not all the items are equally important, but the students will require a basic kit if they are to communicate easily and naturally.

1 Question forms

    a   *Wh-questions*
        What is John doing? Where did he go? etc

    b   *Questions formed with an auxiliary*
        Is John sleeping? Did he have his supper? Can you still see him? etc

    c   *Tag questions*
        John's tired, isn't he? He went home, didn't he? etc
        John didn't see Mary, did he? etc

    d   *Echo questions*
           (John's sleeping.) Sleeping?
           (Mary wears jeans.) Jeans?

    e   *Reversed wh-questions*
           (John went home.) He went where?
           (I met Mary.) You met who?

    f   *Elliptic questions*
           See that? Like to come too?

2 Responses to questions

    a   *Wh-questions*
           What's Mary wearing? Jeans.
           Where did John go? Home.

    b   *Questions formed with an auxiliary and tag questions*
           Is Mary wearing jeans? Yes/No.
                                Yes, she is/No, she isn't.
                                Of course (not).
                                Of course she is/isn't.
                                She is, yes/She isn't, no.*

Other possible responses: I suppose (imagine, think, should think, reckon) she is; I suppose (etc) so; I don't suppose (etc) so; I doubt it.
    Also: maybe, perhaps, probably, obviously.

* This form often indicates some reservation (i.e. Why are you asking me this question?).

3 Responses to statements

    a   *Confirmation*

John likes potatoes.	Yes, he does.
	Yes, he does, doesn't he?
	Of course he does.
	Yes, of course he does.
John doesn't smoke.	No, he doesn't.
	No, he doesn't, does he?
	Of course he doesn't.
	No, of course he doesn't.

    b   *Addition*

Mary wears jeans.	So do I. So does Tom.
	I do too.
	I do as well.

Mary can't swim.	Nor can I. Nor can Tom.
	Neither can I.
	I can't either.
	Nor me.

Note: Many of these forms are exclamatory: So do I! etc

This form provides an important way of expressing personal agreement or disagreement with an opinion, wish, desire etc. For example:

I think he's asleep.	So do I! etc.
I wish I had a car like that.	Well, I don't!
I don't think he's asleep.	Nor do I!
I don't want a drink.	Well, I do!

Notice that in each case the first response expresses agreement and the second one disagreement.

4 Exclamations (examples only)

a   How pretty she is! How lucky they were! What a fool he was!
b   Isn't she pretty! Weren't they lucky!
c   How clever of them! How stupid of me!
d   How (awful)! What a (shame)! Lucky you! You lucky fellow! Poor Mary!
e   Good heavens! Oh, hell! Damn (it)!

Some responses are usually exclamatory:
    Well, that was very pleasant! Yes, wasn't it!
    John's wearing jeans today! So he is!

5 Reported statements

With verbs and phrases such as: I think, imagine, suppose, reckon, guess, take it, am afraid and it seems to me.

Notice: I suppose you're tired.
        You're tired, I suppose.
        It was rather late, I suppose, when you got to bed.

6 Hesitation markers

    Well, maybe he wants a drink.
    Oh, he's trying to climb over the wall.
    Hm, she can't find her hat.
    You know, he looks tired.

7 Opening phrases (examples only)

These also frequently serve as hesitation markers. In general their function is to initiate (further) discussion, acknowledge what the previous speaker has said, and order points of view.

- a By the way, incidentally, as a matter of fact, actually, frankly, personally, seriously (though), in my opinion etc.
- b All the same, that's all very well but, all right (OK) but, I suppose so but, I see your point (agree) but etc.
- c first, next, then, finally, to begin with, for a start, for one thing ... and for another, what's more, from one point of view etc.
- d How about ...? What about ...?

8 Attitudinal adjectives (examples only)

These are also used in exclamations:
wonderful, marvellous, super, great, awful, terrible, rotten, shocking etc.

9 Modifiers (examples only)

- a He *kind of (sort of)* hesitated.
- b It's *a bit* difficult to tell.
- c He *more or less* ignored her.
- d They *practically* ate the lot.
- e I *just (merely, simply)* wanted to say ...

Key to Symbols

[ ] These indicate alternative words or phrases. e.g. begin to cry [burst into tears]

( ) These indicate either words or phrases which may be omitted: e.g. while she has (her) breakfast or which are substitutable. e.g. dictate (a letter) to one's (secretary)

: A colon is used before a list of illustrative items. e.g. electrical goods: vacuum cleaner, TV set etc

Abbreviations
sb. = somebody
sth. = something

Lesson Notes
1

a Useful language

crowd
gather (round)
stand around on the pavement
look [stare, gaze] up in the air
listen open-mouthed
curious [astonished, amazed]

b Guidelines

— who these people are
— how long they have been standing there
— what the man who is pointing has seen
 (someone on the roof/a flying saucer/ . . .)
— whether anyone else has seen it too
— what the man is saying
— whether the others believe him
— what happens after this

c Guided oral exercises

  i A dialogue between the man who is pointing and one or two of the others, to whom he is trying to describe what he saw.
 ii A dialogue between one of the crowd and a passer-by, who wants to know why everyone is standing around.
iii You have just noticed something strange happening (on top of a certain building). Indicate to the person who is with you exactly where to look.

d Discussion

Are you curious by nature? If there is a crowd in the street looking at something, do *you* stop too? What sort of things arouse curiosity?

What is the strangest thing (event) you ever saw?

Do you believe in 'flying saucers'? What is your opinion about them?

2

a Useful language

beach [shore]
get undressed
a (neat) pile of clothes
leave sth. folded up (in a neat pile)

b Guidelines

- who left the clothes on the beach
- where he has gone
  (for a swim/for a run/got drowned/ ...)
- how long they have been there
- whether anyone has seen them
- what will happen if someone sees them

c Guided oral exercises

i A dialogue between two people walking on the beach who come across the clothes.
ii A dialogue between the person who left the clothes on the beach and a friend who is standing there when he comes back.
iii You are walking on the beach (late one evening) when you come across a pile of clothes. You are afraid that the person may have got drowned. Ring up the police and tell them what you have seen and where the clothes are.

d Discussion

Have you ever come across a pile of clothes on the beach — or anything else that seems to have been left there? (What did you do?) How would you react in a situation like this?

What are the beaches like in your country? Can you find beaches that are not crowded? Do you like exploring beaches? What sort of things can you find (washed up) on them?

3

a Useful language

help sb. (to) get up on [over] the wall
climb (up) on (to) sb.'s shoulders
too high to climb over (by oneself)
have a look over the wall

b **Guidelines**
- who the boys are
- why they want to climb over the wall
  (get some fruit/get back a ball/ . . .)
- what they *expect* to find on the other side
- what *is* on the other side
  (orchard/garden/ . . .)
- what happens after this
  (they both climb over/someone catches them/ . . .)

c **Guided oral exercises**
  i A dialogue between the boy on the wall and the other one, talking about what the first one can see.
  ii A dialogue between the first boy and someone on the other side, who is angry because the boy is climbing into his (garden).
  iii You have climbed over a wall into someone's (garden) and the person finds you there. Explain what you are doing there.

d **Discussion**

Have you ever done something like this? (What happened?) Would you climb into someone's (garden)? Would you be angry if the boy climbed into *your* (garden)? What would you say? Suggest different ways of describing these boys' behaviour.

How do people protect their property in your country? (Do they build walls? Do they keep dogs etc?) Is it good to have a strong sense of 'private property'? Why do some people have strong feelings about it?

4

a **Useful language**

parcel [packet], contents

happen to { find sth. (lying) on the pavement
drop sth.
fall out of (a basket)

b **Guidelines**
- who has dropped the parcel
- whether it has been dropped accidentally or left there on purpose
- what is in the parcel
  (something valuable/a present/ . . .)
- who finds the parcel and what he does with it
  (he keeps it/takes it to the police-station/ . . .)

- what consequences this has for the person who has (dropped) the parcel and for the person who finds it

c **Guided oral exercises**
   i A dialogue between two people who find the parcel and discuss what to do about it.
   ii A dialogue between the person who lost the parcel and another person (at home).
   iii You find a parcel in the street and take it to the police-station. Say where and when you found it.

d **Discussion**

Have you ever found a parcel (or anything else) in the street? (What did you do?) What would *you* do if you found a parcel like this? (Would you open it?) Have you ever lost anything (valuable) in the street? (How did it happen? What were the consequences?)

Are people generally honest if they find something? Where do they take 'lost property'? Are there 'lost property offices' in your country?

5

a **Useful language**

pub [bar], barman
have a drink (together)
tell a long [boring] story, boast, exaggerate
laugh at sb. (behind his back)

b **Guidelines**
   - who these people are
   - where they are
   - whether they know one another
   - what the man is telling them
     (an experience in the war/what happened to him on his travels/ . . .)
   - whether the others believe him

c **Guided oral exercises**
   i A dialogue between the bald-headed man, who is boasting about something he did, and the younger man, who keeps interrupting him.
   ii A dialogue between the man on the left and the barman, discussing the other man after he has left.
   iii You want to tell a story but someone keeps interrupting you. Ask the person politely but firmly to stop doing this.

d Discussion

Are you fond of talking? Do you like telling (stories)? When you tell a story about something that happened to you, do you always tell the exact truth? Why do people boast? What sort of things do they boast about? Does the man in the picture remind you of anyone in particular? (Who?)

Where do you go when you want to meet your friends for a chat? Where do people generally meet to talk in your country? Is there any institution like the English 'pub'?

6

a Useful language

typist [secretary], manager [boss]
point out (mistakes)
complain, tell sb. off
begin to cry [burst into tears]

b Guidelines

— who these people are and where (what sort of office) they work in
— what the girl has done wrong
— what the man is saying to her
— what explanation or excuse she gives
— what happens after this

c Guided oral exercises

i A dialogue between the man and the girl, with reference to the mistake(s) she has made in the letter. The girl tries to explain how they occurred.
ii A dialogue between the girl and a friend, to whom she is relating the incident and why it made her cry.
iii You asked someone to type a letter for you and you find that there is a serious mistake in it. Explain carefully what the mistake is and what consequences might result from it.

d Discussion

How would you behave in the man's situation? (Are you patient or do you get angry easily?) If you were the girl, how would you react? How do you generally react if someone tells you off?

Do you (Would you like to) work in an office? What advantages and disadvantages are there about working in an office? Discuss working conditions in an office (salary, hours, holidays etc) and compare these with other occupations.

7

a Useful language

read [study] while she has (her) breakfast
study [work, prepare] for an exam [a test]
bookworm

b Guidelines

- who the girl is
- what she is (studying) and why she is doing it while she has breakfast
- whether she often does this
- how her mother feels
  (annoyed/patient/ . . .)
- what results from this (if she is studying for an exam)

c Guided oral exercises

i A dialogue between the girl and her mother, who disapproves of her daughter doing this.

ii A dialogue between the girl and a friend (over the telephone), discussing how much work they have done for an exam.

iii You have a special reason for reading at table but someone tries to stop you. Explain why it is essential for you to read.

d Discussion

Do you read at table? (Generally or on what occasions?)
Do people (at home) mind? How do you prepare for exams?
(Do you study at the last moment? Do you get good results from this?)

Are examinations necessary? Should they be abolished?
List the good and bad things about examinations.

8

a Useful language

on duty at the police-station
report a theft [robbery, accident]
excited [upset, worked up]

b Guidelines

- who the woman is
- what has happened to her
  (seen an accident/lost her purse/ . . .)

- how the policeman deals with her
- what action he takes

c **Guided oral exercises**

   i A dialogue between the policeman and the woman, who is reporting (an accident) but is confused because she is excited.
   ii A dialogue between the policeman and another one, to whom he is reporting the incident and giving instructions to take action.
   iii You looked out of the window and saw two men (stealing a car). Give as precise a description as you can of the two men.

d **Discussion**

Have you ever had to go to the police-station? (What for?)

Find out as much as you can about policemen. E.g. at what age a person can join the police; what training he gets; how much policemen are paid; what different kinds of jobs are open to them etc.

Decide why you would, or would not, like to be a policeman.

9

a **Useful language**

dictate (a letter) to one's (secretary)
walk [stride] up and down
be in a bad mood [temper]
be angry [irritated, annoyed, upset]

b **Guidelines**

- who the man is and what his position is
  (manager/business executive/...)
- who wrote the letter he has in his hand
- why he is angry
  (someone has broken a contract/cancelled an order/failed to keep an appointment/...)
- how his secretary feels
  (nervous/used to it/...)
- what he says in the letter and what happens as a result

c **Guided oral exercises**

   i A dialogue between the secretary and a friend of hers, talking about the way her boss behaved when he got the letter.
   ii A dialogue between the man and the person who will get this letter, ringing up to protest.
   iii You are the man's secretary. Try to reason with him and persuade him not to write an angry reply.

d Discussion

How would *you* behave in this situation? Have you ever sent someone a letter which you later regretted? Do you lose your temper easily? What are some common situations in which most people get angry or annoyed?

If you were the man's secretary, would you argue with him? Describe the work of a secretary. Would you like to be one?

Look in the newspaper and find out as much as you can about working as a secretary (e.g. training required, positions vacant, salaries).

10

a Useful language

go shopping [window-shopping]
electrical goods: vacuum-cleaner, TV set, transistor, record-player etc
bargain

b Guidelines

- who these people are
  (a married couple/engaged/ . . .)
- what work they do and whether they earn much
- whether they have (a TV) already or want a new one
- how much a new (TV) will cost and whether they can afford it
- what they finally decide to do
- if they decide to buy something, how they pay
  (cash/by cheque/get sth. on hire-purchase/ . . .)

c Guided oral exercises

  i A dialogue between the two people trying to decide whether to buy (a TV).
  ii A dialogue between the salesman in the shop and the couple as he tries to persuade them to buy a (TV).
  iii You are out with a friend and you stop in front of this window. Your friend wants to buy a (new record-player). Find out from your friend whether he really needs it (can afford it etc).

d Discussion

Do you like shopping? Do you like 'window-shopping'?
When you want to buy something, do you take a long time to make up your mind? Which of these items would you like to buy and why?

Are these items common in your country? Are they expensive? (Look in the newspaper and check prices.) Are they made in your country or imported? Do people buy things on hire-purchase?

11

a Useful language

have a quiet evening at home
hear sth. just outside
nervous [puzzled, excited, curious]

b Guidelines
- who these people are and how they have been spending their evening
  (reading/watching TV/knitting/sewing/ . . .)
- what they (think they) have heard
  (someone coming up the path/outside the window/ . . .)
- what their reactions are
- what they say to each other
- whether the man goes out to have a look
- whether this incident affects their evening
  (they call the police/a visitor comes/ . . .)

c Guided oral exercises

i A dialogue between the man and the woman, discussing what they think they have heard.
ii A dialogue between the man and the woman after he has been outside and had a look.
iii You are with a friend in a room and you hear a strange noise outside. He wants (or doesn't want) to go outside and have a look. Persuade him (not) to go.

d Discussion

Have you ever been in a situation similar to this? Were you alone? What happened? What would *you* do in this situation? (Would you go outside and have a look?)
What makes people afraid (nervous) in situations like this?

12

a Useful language

maps
discuss [make, go over] plans (for a holiday)
decide on [work out] a route [places to visit]

9

b Guidelines
- who these boys are
  (brothers/school-friends/ ...)
- what they are looking at
- what they are planning to do
- what happens as a result of this meeting

c Guided oral exercises
  i A dialogue between the two boys arranging the meeting over the phone, with one of them reminding the other which maps to bring.
  ii A dialogue between the two boys trying to agree on a suitable place for their holiday.
  iii You learn that two friends are planning to spend their holiday in a certain place which you know but they do not. Dissuade them from going and suggest an alternative place.

d Discussion

How do you arrange your holiday? Do you plan it carefully? Do (Would) you prefer to go alone or with (friends)?
What was the best holiday you ever had?

Work out three or four different ways of having a holiday and compare their advantages and disadvantages.

13

a Useful language

look surprised [amazed, astonished, astounded]

b Guidelines
- who the man is
- who has written the letter
  (his bank manager/a person asking for money/a friend he has not seen for a long time/ ...)
- whether he knows who has written the letter
- how he feels
- what he does as a result of getting the letter

c Guided oral exercises
  i A dialogue between the man and (his wife), whom he is telling about the letter.
  ii A dialogue between the man and the person who wrote the letter (perhaps in the form of a telephone conversation).
  iii Someone has written you a very (unkind) letter. Tell him how you feel.

d Discussion

Have you ever got a letter which (surprised) you? What about? What did you do? Have you ever written anyone a letter which (annoyed) him? What happened as a result?

You have to tell someone something unpleasant: would you write him a letter or ring him up? Consider the advantages and disadvantages of these two ways of communicating with the person.

14

a Useful language

ask the way
tell sb. how to get to [give sb. directions]
help sb. to find the way to a place

b Guidelines
— who the man is
  (foreigner/tourist/visitor/stranger/new to a place/ . . .)
— where he wants to go and why he wants to go there
— whether he is lost
— what he asks the policeman
— what the policeman says

c Guided oral exercises
  i A dialogue between the policeman and the man, who is a stranger to the town looking for a (good cheap restaurant).
  ii A dialogue between the policeman and yourself (as the man in the street), asking the way to the (railway station).
  iii Imagine that you are (outside the railway station) and someone asks you the way to (the hospital). Give precise instructions how to get there.

d Discussion

Have you helped someone in a situation like this? Tell us about it. Have you ever been lost? (What happened? Who did you ask?)

Is it easy to give directions? What is important when giving directions? Are policemen helpful in your country? Can they usually speak more than one language?

Look at a map of your city (town). Is it up-to-date and accurate? If there are several maps of the city, compare them and see in what respects they are better than one another.

15

a **Useful language**

apply for a job [post, appointment] as
applicant, [candidate], (members of the) board
go for an interview, be interviewed

b **Guidelines**

- who the young man is
- why he is being interviewed
  (a job/oral examination/...)
- what questions he is being asked
- how he feels
- what the members of the board think of him
- how he feels after the interview
- what the members of the board decide

c **Guided oral exercises**

i A dialogue between the secretary of the board and the young man, arranging the appointment for the interview over the phone.
ii A dialogue between members of the board discussing the applicant after the interview.
iii You have just been interviewed for a job as a (reporter). Ring up a friend and tell him how the interview went.

d **Discussion**

Have you ever been in a situation like this one? (For a job or an oral examination.) Do you feel nervous on occasions like this? (Why?)

Is an interview a good way of finding out what people are like? (What about oral examinations?)

Imagine that you had to choose someone to work for you. What qualities would you look for?

16

a **Useful language**

wait for sb. to arrive [come back]
get off (a plane)
get nervous [excited, worked up]
on time, delayed [held up]

b **Guidelines**
- who the woman is
- how long she has been waiting and whether the plane is on time
- who she is waiting for
- where the person is coming from
  (*returning from a holiday/business trip/ ...*)
- if the person has been away, how long he has been away
- if he is arriving for the first time, how long he will stay
- what they talk about when they meet

c **Guided oral exercises**
  i A dialogue between the woman and the boy with her. The woman can see the person they are waiting for but the child cannot.
  ii Between the woman and the person who has arrived, discussing the flight and (his trip abroad).
  iii You are waiting for someone to arrive by air. Ring up the reception desk at the airport, give full details of the person and the flight and ask for a certain message to be given to him.

d **Discussion**

Do you often go (Have you ever been) to the airport to meet someone? Do you get anxious if the flight is delayed? Do you like travelling by air?

What are the advantages and disadvantages of air travel for holidays (business trips etc)? What places can you fly to in your country? Compare cost and time with travelling by train to any one place.

17

a **Useful language**

clerk, post office, stamps
have [get] a parcel weighed
send a parcel off
by air [sea] mail

b **Guidelines**
- who the woman is
- what is in the parcel
  (*food/clothes/books/ ...*)
- who she is sending it to and where the person lives
  (*in the same country/abroad/ ...*)
- how much it weighs
- how often she sends parcels (to this person)

c **Guided oral exercises**
  i A dialogue between the woman and the post office clerk, with details of how much it will cost to send the parcel and how long it will take to arrive.
  ii A dialogue between the person who receives the parcel and another, discussing what might be in the parcel as they open it.
  iii A person gives you a parcel to post which you think is badly wrapped. Explain to the person what might happen if the parcel is sent like this, and how it should be wrapped up.

d **Discussion**
How long does it take for a parcel to reach your country from England? How are they usually sent? (By air or by surface mail?) Give some information about the postal service in your country (e.g. the working hours, how often letters and parcels are delivered, how they are delivered etc).

18

a **Useful language**
go through [turn out, empty out] one's pockets

b **Guidelines**
  - who the boy is
  - why he is turning out his pockets
    (he has lost/borrowed sth./ ...)
  - whether he is alone
  - whether he finds what is missing
  - what will happen if it is not found

c **Guided oral exercises**
  i A dialogue between the boy and another person, referring to what has been lost and what the consequences will be if it is not found.
  ii A dialogue between the man and a friend, who has lost something and insists on seeing whether his friend has put it in his pocket by mistake.
  iii When you arrive home, you find that you have picked up and put in your (bag) by mistake something belonging to a friend. Ring up and say what has happened and explain how it might have occurred.

d Discussion

Have you ever picked up something belonging to another person by mistake? (How did it happen? Was he annoyed about it?)

If you suspected that someone had taken your (pen), how would you try to find out?

Which of your possessions do you value the most? Why? What precautions do you take to see that it does not get lost or stolen?

19

a Useful language

go [take, invite sb.] out for a meal
(first) course
advise sb. to have (soup)
recommend [suggest] sth.

b Guidelines

- who the man is and who is with him
  (his wife/a (girl) friend/a business acquaintance/ . . .)
- which meal they are having
  (lunch/dinner)
- why they have come to the restaurant and what it is like
- what the man is saying
- what they finally order

c Guided oral exercises

i A dialogue between the man and the person who is with him, discussing what to have as a (first) course.
ii You have invited (a friend) to have dinner with you in a restaurant which you know well. Advise (your friend) what to have.
iii You are with someone in a restaurant and you cannot decide what to eat. Ask the waiter's advice.

d Discussion

Do you like eating out in restaurants? Do you do it very often? Which is your favourite restaurant? Is it (cheap)? What is your favourite dish?

Are there many restaurants in your (town)? Do people eat out a lot?

Make a list of two or three good restaurants in your (town). Give their addresses and telephone numbers, and directions on how to get there. Say approximately how much a good meal would cost.

20

a **Useful language**

desert island, horizon
survivor [castaway]
shipwrecked [marooned, washed ashore]
to be rescued

b **Guidelines**
- who the man is
- how he has come to be on the desert island
- how long he has been there
- how he generally passes the time
- what he is thinking as he sees the ship on the horizon
- whether he is going to do anything
  (shout/light a fire/...)

c **Guided oral exercises**
  i A dialogue between two people on the ship, looking in the direction of the island and wondering what life would be like on it.
  ii A dialogue between the man and someone in the boat which comes to rescue him.
  iii You are on a desert island and some people come to rescue you. Explain why you do not want to go back to civilisation.

d **Discussion**

What would you do in this situation? How would you attract attention? Would you *want* to attract attention? How would you spend you time on a desert island?
Do you mind (like) being alone?

Give an account of any survival story you have read.

Note: Game 60 may be played as follow-up.

21

a **Useful language**

rush [dash] at top speed [as fast as you can]
run for the train
just miss the train (by a few seconds)

b **Guidelines**
- who the young man is
- why he is late
- why he wants to catch this train
- whether he still hopes to catch it
- how long he has to wait for the next one
- what happens as a result of his missing the train

c **Guided oral exercises**
   i A dialogue between the young man and the porter, discussing the next best train to catch.
   ii A dialogue between two of the young man's friends, discussing his absence (at the office) that morning.
   iii You have just missed a train, which will prevent you from (keeping an appointment). Ring up and explain what has happened, and why, and say when you expect to arrive.

d **Discussion**

Has this ever happened to you? (Why? What were the consequences?) Do you always allow plenty of time when you have to go to the (station) to catch a (train)? What sort of things can hold you up on the way?

Decide on a city which you would like to visit. Then consult a timetable or ring up the station to find out what the possibilities are, and choose the train which suits you best.

22

a **Useful language**

reporter [journalist], photographer
to interview sb.
ask for [make] a statement

b **Guidelines**
- who the man coming down the steps is
  (a VIP/politician/lawyer/ . . .)
- what he has been doing
- what the reporter asks him
- what he replies
- whether he is willing or unwilling (to make a statement)
- what the reporter does after this

c **Guided oral exercises**

   i A dialogue between the reporter and the man, who has just come out of an important meeting.
   ii A dialogue between the reporter and the editor of his paper, giving him the news over the phone.
   iii You are a reporter. Try to persuade (a famous person) to give you an interview.

d **Discussion**

Would you like to be a newspaper reporter? What kind of reporter would you like to be? (e.g. sports, political events, crimes)

What kind of training does a newspaper reporter need to have? What qualities does a good reporter need?

Look at your national newspapers. Decide which give the best reports. Which do you think is the best newspaper or the one you prefer reading? Give reasons.

23

a **Useful language**

get into a house through a window
break [force] open a window
locked out

b **Guidelines**

— who the man is
— whose house this is
— why he is forcing open the window
— why there is no one in the house
— whether anyone sees him
— what he does next

c **Guided oral exercises**

   i A dialogue between the man and a policeman, who asks him what he is doing.
   ii A dialogue between the man and a friend, to whom he is explaining what he had to do when he arrived without his keys and found no one in the house.
   iii You were invited to stay with a friend but when you arrived at his house, you found him out. You decided to climb in through a window, but while you were doing so, a neighbour saw you. Explain yourself.

d Discussion

Have you ever had to do something like this? Would you do it if you had to?

This is a typically English house (with a downstairs and an upstairs). What are the houses in your country like? Are flats more common? How would you get into a flat if you didn't have the key?

24

a Useful language

come [get] home late
keep sb. waiting [up late]
make an excuse
cross [annoyed, upset]

b Guidelines

— who these people are
— how long the woman has been waiting
— why the man is late
(worked late in the office/been to a meeting/the pub/ . . .)
— what excuse the man makes
— how his wife feels and what she says to her husband

c Guided oral exercises

i A dialogue between the woman, who is angry because her husband is late, and the man, who makes excuses.
ii A dialogue between the woman and (a friend), discussing this the next day over the phone.
iii You arrive late for an appointment and your friend is very cross. Explain why you are late and try to pacify him.

d Discussion

What excuse would you make in this man's position?
Have you ever arrived late (for an appointment)? What happened?
Are people in your country generally punctual? Discuss the question of punctuality in relation to daily and professional life. (What are the reasons for not being punctual? What bad results does it have?)

25

a **Useful language**

(football) match, game, players
knock(ed) down, badly hurt [injured], broken (leg)
to be carried off [taken away] on a stretcher
interrupt the game

b **Guidelines**

- what match they are playing and where
- how the accident happened
- what happens to the injured players
- how the crowd reacts
- what effect the incident has on the game

c **Guided oral exercises**

i A dialogue between the injured player who is holding his leg and the man standing beside him.
ii A dialogue between two spectators discussing the incident.
iii You are a friend of the player who is being taken away on a stretcher. Ring up the man's wife, tell her what has happened and which hospital to go to.

d **Discussion**

Do you play football? (Did you ever play? Were you ever hurt? What happened?)

Is football very popular in your country? Do you watch it? (On TV?)

Make some notes on your favourite (or any important) football team. E.g. who the captain and important players are; which games they have played this season and where; whether they have won etc. Has the team suffered any serious accidents like this one? If so, describe it.

26

a **Useful language**
milkman, horse and cart
deliver the milk
have the milk delivered

b **Guidelines**
- what has happened to the milkman
- what the woman thinks when she opens her door
- what she does
- what she says to the horse
- what she says to the milkman (when he turns up)

c **Guided oral exercises**
   i A dialogue between the woman and the milkman, who explains where he has been.
   ii A dialogue between the woman and (her husband), to whom she relates the incident when he comes home.
   iii You happened to look out of your window and you saw a strange incident (like this one) in the street. Ring up a friend and tell him about it.

d **Discussion**

Have you ever seen a strange incident like this? What would you do if this happened to you?

Is milk delivered to the house in your country? How? What are horses still used for in your country? What are the advantages and disadvantages of using horses for transport?

Discuss any of the delivery services available in your country. Describe how it is organised (how often and what it costs) and whether it is efficient.

27

a **Useful language**
postbox
post a letter
on the point of [just about to]
hesitate
try to make up one's mind whether to

b **Guidelines**
- who the woman is
- who she has written to
  (a relative/friend/ . . .)
- what she has written in the letter
- why she is hesitating
  (worried/not satisfied/ . . .)
- whether she finally decides to post the letter
- what will happen if she posts (doesn't post) the letter

c **Guided oral exercises**

   i A dialogue in the form of a telephone conversation between the woman and the person who gets the letter.
   ii A dialogue in the form of a telephone conversation between the woman and the person who was expecting the letter but did not get it.
   iii You are walking along the street and you see a friend hesitating whether to post a letter. Find out tactfully the reason for this.

d **Discussion**

   Have you ever written a letter and then decided not to send it? Why? Have you ever regretted sending a letter? What were the consequences? Do you write to lots of people? (Do you do this because you like to or because you have to? Do you have pen-friends? Where?) Are letters a good form of communication?

28

a **Useful language**

   elderly, retired
   old-age pensioners
   argue [chat, gossip, pass the time (of day)]

b **Guidelines**

   − who these old men are
   − where they are
   − whether they often meet here
   − how long they have known each other
   − what they usually talk about
   − what they are talking about now

c **Guided oral exercises**

   i A dialogue between the two old men, describing the event which is suggested by the second picture.
   ii A dialogue between the two old men, discussing, for example, how difficult it is for them to live on the money they get.
   iii You are a journalist. You want to write an article about one of the men. Ask him questions about himself (e.g. his name, age, what work he did, whether he lives by himself, how he passes the time etc.)

d **Discussion**

   How would you like to spend *your* old age?

At what age do people generally retire in your country? Do they get pensions? Are there clubs and other facilities for them? How do they generally spend their time?

Find out as much as you can about conditions for old people (e.g. what pensions they get, what happens to them if they have no relatives etc). Read a newspaper to see what articles and reports there are on them.

29

a **Useful language**

platform [stage], (political) meeting [debate]
make [deliver] a speech
make sb. think [laugh]
feel nervous [excited]

b **Guidelines**

- who the young man is
- where he is speaking
  (political meeting/school debate/ ...)
- what he is speaking about
- how many people are listening to him
- whether he is making a good speech
- how he feels
- how the audience reacts to his speech

c **Guided oral exercises**

i A dialogue between the speaker and one of the other people on the stage, praising or criticising the speech.
ii A dialogue between two members of the audience, talking about the various speeches.
iii You are asked to make a speech at short notice, but you do not want to. Make an excuse.

d **Discussion**

Have you ever made a speech? Did you feel nervous? What was the speech about? Was it a good speech? Did people clap afterwards?

Are there any clubs (societies) in your school? Which ones involve speaking in public? Are they popular?

Which careers involve speaking in public? Would you like to be a (politician)?

Who is the politician you like most? Is he a good speaker? What qualities do you expect in a good public speaker?

30

a **Useful language**

police, police-car
make enquiries
arrest [take away] sb.

b **Guidelines**

- who lives in the house
- why the police have come there
- who opens the door
- what they say
- what happens after that

c **Guided oral exercises**

  i A dialogue between the two policemen, discussing what to do because no one answers the door.
  ii A dialogue between one of the policemen and the (man's wife), who comes to the door. The policeman tries to find out where the (man) is without explaining what he wants.
  iii You open the door to find two policemen there who are making enquiries about (a friend of yours). Tell the police when you last saw him and where they might expect to find him.

d **Discussion**

What are the police like in your country? Do people like them? Are they afraid of them?

Are there different kinds of police in your country? If so, what are they and what are their functions? What kind of uniforms do they wear?

31

a **Useful language**

(reference) library, book stacks, catalogues
top [bottom] shelf
librarian, (library) assistant
look sth. up in [consult] a reference book

b **Guidelines**

- who the young man is
- what subject he is studying (interested in)

- whether the (reference) library is a good one and what it contains
- whether many, and what kind of, people use it
- what book the young man is looking for
- whether he has already tried to find it
- what the assistant says to him

c **Guided oral exercises**

   i A dialogue between the (student) and the librarian, with details of the book the (student) wants and where he can find it.

   ii You want three books on (history). Ask the librarian for these (giving titles and authors), enquiring first whether they are available and then where they can be found.

   iii A friend wants to read up e.g. a certain period in (literature). Suggest some suitable books and where he can find or get them.

d **Discussion**

   Is there a (reference) library in your (city)? Is it a good one? Do you use it? (What for?) Is it a good place to work in? Do you generally buy books or borrow them from a library?

   Find out what you can about a career as a librarian. E.g. how they are trained and for how long; what they earn etc. Then decide whether you would like to work as a librarian, giving reasons for and against.

32

a **Useful language**

   canteen [cafe, restaurant]
   talk [gossip] about
   take no notice of [ignore, not aware of]

b **Guidelines**
   - who and where these people are
   - what the girls are saying about the young man
   - whether they know him personally and whether he knows them
   - whether he is aware that they are talking about him and whether he cares
   - whether he stops to say anything

c **Guided oral exercises**

   i A dialogue between the two girls in which one of them tells some story about the young man.

   ii A dialogue between the young man and the two girls. He interrupts them and accuses them (angrily or in fun) of gossiping about him and they deny it.

iii Someone has been gossiping about you and you find out. Explain to the person what trouble this has caused you.

d Discussion

What would you do if you were the young man? Would you take any notice if you knew that the girls were talking about you? Do you gossip about people? Why do people gossip?

Which newspapers or journals in your country contain a lot of gossip? What sort of people do they write about? Find an example of gossiping in a newspaper ór magazine and relate the incident. Do you think it was true?

33

a Useful language

workman: plumber, electrician, carpenter
mend [repair, fix]
get sth. (mended)

b Guidelines

- who the young man is
- what (precisely) he has come to do
- how the woman feels
  (pleased because he has come/angry because he is late/ . . .)
- what happens next

c Guided oral exercises

i A dialogue between the woman, who is cross because the (plumber) should have come the day before, and the young man, who explains why he could not come, or makes excuses.
ii You have called a workman to your house to do or repair something. Explain exactly what you want done.
iii You open your door to find a workman there whom you have not sent for, and you are suspicious. Try to find out exactly what he wants.

d Discussion

Do people in your country generally (try to) repair things for themselves? What sort of things can you repair? Were you taught to do that (at school) or did you learn by yourself? Are (plumbers) reliable in your country? Do they charge a lot?

Think about the life of (an electrician) who works for himself. What advantages and disadvantages are there in working in this way (compared, say, with working in a factory)? Find out what you can about how (electricians) are trained, the different kinds of work they can do and how much they earn.

34

a **Useful language**

refuse to buy sb. (a coat)
too dear [expensive]
mean, short of money
not in stock [available]
upset, sulky

b **Guidelines**

— what the girl wanted
— whether the (mother) refused to buy it for her and if so, why
— whether what the girl wanted was available
  (the wrong size/too big/too small/ . . .)
— how they feel

c **Guided oral exercises**

  i A dialogue between the daughter, who wants a very expensive or modish (dress), and the (mother), who does not want to buy it.
  ii A dialogue between the woman and her husband, whom she is telling about the incident later.
  iii You want to buy a certain article (item of clothing, jewellery). Convince the person who is with you why you must have it.

d **Discussion**

Have you had an experience like this? Tell us about it. If you were the (daughter), how would *you* react? Do you sympathise with both the (mother) and the (daughter)? State the case for each of them.

Are clothes very expensive in your country? If so, why? Where are they made?

Make a list of the things which are in fashion at the moment and compare these with the ones which were in fashion (two or three years ago).

35

a Useful language

wait for sb. (to come out)
plain-clothes [private] detective
keep a watch [an eye on]
pretend to (read the paper)

b Guidelines

- who the young man is and why he is waiting
  (a detective/thief/someone's boy-friend/ ...)
- how long he has been waiting
- whether anyone has noticed him
- what finally happens

c Guided oral exercises

i A dialogue between the man and someone who comes out of the block of flats and asks him what he is doing there.
ii You have been waiting for your (girl-friend) outside in the street for an hour. Ring up and find out what has happened.
iii You are in the block of flats and have noticed this young man waiting outside all morning. Ring up the police, reporting the matter. Describe the person and the place.

d Discussion

Are you patient when you have to wait for someone? How do you generally pass the time?

Would you like to be a detective? Do you think they have an interesting or exciting life? What qualities do you associate with them?

36

a Useful language

go away on holiday
put (the luggage) in (the back of) the car
help (to) load the car
lend a hand

b Guidelines

- who these people are
- where they are going

- how long they will spend there
- what they are taking with them (as luggage)
- whether there are any problems connected with their leaving
(too much luggage/how to arrange it/ . . .)

c **Guided oral exercises**
  i A dialogue between the man and the boy about the best way to arrange all the luggage.
  ii A dialogue between the man and his wife because there is too much luggage and something has to be left behind.
  iii You are about to leave for a week's holiday with a friend (at the seaside). Question him to find out whether all the essential things have been packed.

d **Discussion**

How do you like to travel when you go on holiday? What are the advantages and disadvantages of taking a car on holiday?

You can only take one small suitcase with you for a week's holiday (at the seaside). What will you take?

You are going to spend ten days touring a certain part of your country by car. Work out a plan for your holiday e.g. which places you must visit and how long you will spend in each; which places you will visit if you have time; which routes you will follow and how far you will have to travel.

37

a **Useful language**

tape-recorder
teach yourself by listening to tapes
repeat [imitate], memorise [learn by heart]

b **Guidelines**
  - who the boy is
  - what he is studying
  - if he is learning a language, which one
  - why he is studying on his own
    (for an exam/to go abroad/ . . .)
  - how long he has been studying
  - how often he studies
  - whether he enjoys doing it
  - how much progress he has made

c **Guided oral exercises**

   i A dialogue between the boy and someone who comes into the room and interrupts him.
   ii A friend wants to study (French) on his own. Advise him how to go about it.
   iii Persuade a friend who wants to learn (French) to learn (German) instead.

d **Discussion**

Have you ever tried to learn a language with the help of a (tape-recorder)? Were you successful? What are some of the advantages and disadvantages?

Do more people want to learn languages nowadays? Why? Which foreign languages are popular in your country?

List and discuss some of the reasons why people want to learn a foreign language.

38

a **Useful language**

happen to (look out of the window)
see sb. doing sth.
tell sb. to come and (have a look)

b **Guidelines**

- what she has seen
  (action/event/...)
- whether it is amusing (exciting, disturbing etc)
- where the (event) is taking place
  (in the garden/street/...)
- who else is in the room and what (they are) doing
- what the woman says
- whether the other person comes and has a look too

c **Guided oral exercises**

   i A dialogue between the woman and another person in the room about what is happening outside the window.
   ii You look out of the window and see something happening which you think is (amusing). Try to arouse the interest of someone else who is in the room and persuade him to come and have a look too.
   iii You look out of the window and you see some men fighting or an accident in the street. Phone the police.

d Discussion

Why do people like looking out of windows? What sort of people do it mostly? Do you spend much time looking out of the window? Have you ever looked out of the window and seen something (exciting)? Tell us about it.

39

a Useful language

present
opened [unwrapped, tore the paper off] the parcel
thrilled [delighted] with
excited about

b Guidelines

— who these people are
— what occasion it is
 (birthday/Christmas/ . . .)
— what is in the parcel
— where they bought it and how much it cost
— what the girl says as she opens the parcel
— what she does with her present

c Guided oral exercises

  i A dialogue between the parents, discussing what to buy their daughter for (her birthday).
 ii A dialogue between the parents and their daughter. She is trying to guess what is in the parcel before she opens it.
iii You have bought an unsuitable present for a friend and you want to change it for something else. Explain the situation to the shop assistant.

d Discussion

How do you choose presents for people? Is it better to find out first what they would like or need? How would you do this? Why do people give presents? Do you like getting them? What was the best (worst, strangest) present you ever got?

On what occasions do people give presents in your country? In many countries the custom of giving presents on certain occasions has been commercialised. Has this happened in your country too?

40

a **Useful language**

wait at the bus-stop
just miss a bus
a bus (every half-hour)
get worried [worked up, desperate]

b **Guidelines**

- who the man is, where he is going and for how long
- what he has in his suitcase
- how often there is a bus and whether he has *just* missed one
- what he decides to do next
  (wait for the next one/call a taxi/walk/ ...)
- what effect missing the bus will have on his plans
- whether the two men at the bus-stop know each other
- whether they begin to talk

c **Guided oral exercises**

  i A dialogue between the two men complaining about the poor bus service.
  ii A dialogue between the two men, with the first making reference to the effect it will have on his plans because he has missed the bus.
  iii You arrive at the bus-stop to find that a bus has just left. Find out from someone how often the bus goes to the (station), whether there is only one bus service and whether it is possible to get a taxi.

d **Discussion**

Have you ever been in a situation like this (when you were in a hurry and you just missed a bus)? What did you do?

What is the bus service like in your (city)? Is it reliable (regular, cheap)? Do most people use it or do they prefer to use their cars?

41

a **Useful language**

doctor's (house, surgery), (door) bell
try hard to ring the bell
(can) just manage to reach the bell by standing on tiptoe

b **Guidelines**
- who the girl is
- who has sent her
- why she has been sent
- how long she has to wait
- what happens after she rings the bell

c **Guided oral exercises**
   i A dialogue between the girl and the person who sent her, giving her the message and telling her exactly where to go and what to do.
   ii A dialogue between the girl and the person who opens the door.
   iii You are a passer-by and you see that the girl is upset because she cannot reach the doorbell. Find out what the matter is and comfort her as you help her.

d **Discussion**

How do you get medical help in an emergency in your country? Can you go to the doctor's house or must you go to the hospital? Where do doctors have their surgeries — at home or in a separate place? Which do you think is better?

What is the medical service like in your country? Are there enough doctors? Is medical attention free?

42

a **Useful language**

fireplace
kneel
about to set light [put a match] to
get rid of [destroy] by burning

b **Guidelines**
- who the man is
- what he is going to burn
  (letters/bills/secret papers/ . . .)
- why he is doing this
- what he thinks as he does this
- what happens as a result of this

c **Guided oral exercises**
   i A dialogue between the man and a person who comes into the room and is (surprised) to see what he is doing.

ii A dialogue between the man and a person who tries to persuade him not to destroy the (papers).
iii You discover that someone has (thrown away) some (letters) which you wanted to keep. Tell the person off, explaining why you wanted to keep the (letters).

d **Discussion**

Do you tend to keep old letters (papers)? Why? How do you store them? Do you sort them out from time to time? Have you ever (thrown away) (papers) which you afterwards wanted? What made you do it?

43

a **Useful language**

(tele)phone box [kiosk]
queue
ring sb. up, make a long distance call
keep sb. waiting
unaware [indifferent, selfish]

b **Guidelines**

— who the girl in the phone box is
— who she is talking to and what she is talking about
— how long she has been talking
— whether she is aware, or cares, that people are waiting
— how each person in the queue feels
— whether anyone does anything
  (interrupts her by opening the door/tapping on the window/...)

c **Guided oral exercises**

i A dialogue between the girl and the person she is talking to on the phone, bringing the conversation to an end because she has noticed the queue outside.
ii A dialogue between any two people in the queue, complaining about the girl in the phone box.
iii You are waiting outside a phone box for someone to finish talking but he goes on for a long time. You have to phone urgently. Interrupt the person, giving your reasons.

d **Discussion**

Would *you* interrupt the girl? How would you do it? Suggest reasons why each person in the queue wants to phone.

Where are the public telephones in your country? Are they sufficient? Are they expensive?

44

a **Useful language**

stretcher
to be taken ill, have an accident
send for an ambulance
to take [be taken] away to hospital

b **Guidelines**

- who is being taken to hospital
- what is wrong with the person and how serious it is
  (heart attack/pneumonia/...)
- how the other people feel
- what happens to the person in hospital

c **Guided oral exercises**

i A dialogue between two people (in the house next door or in the street) who see this incident and wonder what has happened.
ii You have just seen a (man) taken ill in the street. Phone for an ambulance, explaining why and where you need it.
iii A friend of yours is in hospital. Ring up to find out how he is.

d **Discussion**

Have you ever seen an incident like this? What was wrong with the person? (Had he been taken ill or had an accident?) Have you ever had to send for an ambulance? What for? Have you ever been taken to hospital in an ambulance? (What was wrong with you?)

Find out about the ambulance service in your country. E.g. how to get an ambulance; how much it costs; whether it is a good service etc.

45

a **Useful language**

customs (officer, check)
go through customs
open up a suitcase
sth. to declare
smuggle

b **Guidelines**
- who the man is
- where he has come from
- what he has in his suitcase
- whether he has anything to declare
- what he is thinking
- what the customs officer is thinking
- what happens after he has opened up his suitcase

c **Guided oral exercises**
  i A dialogue between customs officer and the man, first asking him to open the suitcase and then discussing certain items in it.
  ii A dialogue between the man and his wife, with reference to the customs check.
  iii On your return from abroad, a customs officer asks you if you have anything to declare. You have three items. Tell him what they are, where you bought them and how much you paid for them.

d **Discussion**

Do you go abroad very often? Do you usually bring many things back with you? What sort of things? Do you declare them when you go through customs? Have you ever smuggled anything? How do you feel when you pass through customs? Is the check very strict? What are you allowed to take into your country without paying duty?

Would you like to be a customs officer?

Find out as much as you can about the work of a customs officer.

46

a **Useful language**

put a notice [an announcement] up (on a notice-board)
information about

b **Guidelines**
- what the notice is about
- how many people it will interest
- what will result from the notice being put up

c **Guided oral exercises**
  i A dialogue between two of the boys discussing the information contained in the notice.

ii You have seen a notice (about a meeting) but you think there is a mistake in it. Speak to the person who wrote the notice to establish whether the information is correct or not.
iii You have just seen a very important notice on the (school) notice board. Tell (a friend) what it is about.

d Discussion

Do you have meetings in your school? How are they announced? Is there a notice-board? (Where is it?) Is it used a lot? Can anyone put up notices there? What kind of notices can you find on it? How often do you go there to read them?

You have to write out a notice announcing a meeting of some kind. Explain how you would set it out and what kind of details you would include.

47

a Useful language

just as sb. is about to leave [on the point of going out]
in a hurry
made up, dressed up
annoyed [cross, exasperated]
bother! damn! blast!

b Guidelines

— who the woman is
— why she is dressed up and where she is going
  (to a party/to meet a friend/ . . .)
— what the woman thinks when the phone rings
— whether she answers the phone and if so, what she says
— who has rung up and what the person wants
— what effect if any the phone call has on her plans

c Guided oral exercises

i A dialogue between the person who has rung up and the woman, trying to conceal her eagerness to leave.
ii A dialogue between the person who has rung up and the woman, whom the caller tries to persuade to change her plans.
iii Someone rings you up just as you are in a hurry to go out or are very busy. Explain to the person why you have not got time to talk.

d Discussion

Has something like this ever happened to you? What did you do? If you were the woman, what would *you* do?

Is it essential (desirable) to have a phone at home? In what ways is a phone especially useful? What effect do phones have on your daily life?

Make a list of the things for which you use the phone in your everyday life and put these in order of importance. Discuss both the advantages and disadvantages of having a phone at home.

48

a **Useful language**

businessman [executive, manager, consultant]
heavy [busy] day
lots of appointments [engagements]
show sb. in (to the office)
shake hands

b **Guidelines**

— who the man is
— what firm he works for
— what position he holds
— who has come to see him
— what the meeting is about
— what happens as a result of the meeting

c **Guided oral exercises**

i A dialogue between the man and his secretary, announcing the arrival of the visitor, who has no appointment but is rather important.

ii A dialogue between the man and his visitor, with exchange of greetings and a brief reference to the business to be discussed.

iii You are acting as someone's secretary. Tell him about his engagements for the following (morning), giving a few details about each.

d **Discussion**

Would you like to work as a business (executive)? Why? Do you think they *really* enjoy life? Have you talked to men like this about their work? Do they enjoy the work or 'success'?

What are the important industries in your country? Which ones produce goods for export?

38

49

a **Useful language**

meet for coffee [tea]
talk [chat, gossip] about sb.

b **Guidelines**

— who the women are
— which woman has invited them
— how often they meet
— what they usually talk about
— what they are talking about now

c **Guided oral exercises**

  i A dialogue between the woman in the centre, who is telling a story about someone, and the others, who interrupt her to ask questions or make comments.
  ii A dialogue between the woman on the left and the woman on the right, talking about their hostess as they go home.
  iii You want to invite someone to your house for (tea) to meet another friend. Ring the person up and tell him when to come and who he will meet.

d **Discussion**

Why do people spend their time in this way? Do women gossip more than men?

Where do women usually meet in your country? How do they pass the time?

Do many women work in your country? What careers are open to them?

Compare this picture with picture 55.

50

a **Useful language**

try to get in at a hotel
full [booked] up, all rooms taken, no rooms free
no room until

39

b **Guidelines**
- who the young man is
- where he has come from and why he is travelling
- whether he has booked a room
- whether the receptionist has (or wants to give him) a room
- how the young man feels
- what he says
- what he does after this

c **Guided oral exercises**
  i A dialogue between the young man and the receptionist, who explains why there are no rooms available but tells him where he might find one.
  ii You arrive at a hotel and you enquire about a room. Say exactly what sort of room you would like, how long you would like it for and find out how much it will cost.
  iii You have not been able to get in at a hotel. Ring up (a friend), explain your position and find out whether he will put you up.

d **Discussion**

Do you travel a lot? Where do you usually stay? Do you book beforehand if you want to stay in a hotel? Has something like this ever happened to you (or someone you know)? (What did you do?) How would you help someone in a situation like this?

Someone has asked you to recommend a hotel which is good but reasonably priced. Decide from among the hotels in your (city) which one(s) would be suitable and find out how much it would cost to stay for a week, what facilities it has etc.

51

a **Useful language**
stay up [wait up] late
wait for sb. to (come home)
tired (out)
in a bad temper [mood]

b **Guidelines**
- who the man is
- who he is waiting up for
  (his son/daughter/ . . .)
- when he usually goes to bed
- how he feels
- why the person he is waiting for is late
- what they say to each other when the person arrives

c **Guided oral exercises**

　i A dialogue between the man and his (son). The father is angry; the (son) explains why he is late and tries to pacify (his) father.
　ii A dialogue between the man and his wife, relating what happened when their (daughter) got home. The wife defends the (daughter).
　iii You arrive home late and your (father) is very angry. Explain why you are late.

d **Discussion**

Have you ever got home very late? Where had you been? What made you late? What time are you generally expected to be home? Are your parents strict? Do you argue with them? How would you behave towards your children if you were a parent?

Discuss the 'generation-gap'. What are the principal differences (in behaviour, views, dress etc) between parents and children?

52

a **Useful language**

court, magistrate
young offender [juvenile delinquent]
commit a crime [robbery, theft]
arrest, accuse, sentence
find sb. (not) guilty
dismiss a charge

b **Guidelines**

— who the boy is
— what the clerk of the court is saying about him
— whether he actually committed the offence
— whether he has been in trouble before
— how he feels
— what will happen to him

c **Guided oral exercises**

　i A dialogue between one of the magistrates and the boy, who is protesting his innocence.
　ii A dialogue between two people who know the boy and who were in court at the time.
　iii You are accused of causing a disturbance in the street. Give your version of what happened.

d Discussion

Do young people often break the law? What sort of offences do they commit? What happens to them if they are found guilty?

Is juvenile crime increasing? If so, what do you think the reasons are?

Have you ever paid a visit to a court? What was happening at the time?

Explain the system of courts in your country and comment on it.

53

a Useful language

eat (out) on one's own [by oneself]
self-service cafe [restaurant]

b Guidelines
- who the boy is
- where he is eating
- what he is eating
  (steak and chips/fish and chips/ ...)
- why he is eating on his own
- what he is looking at and thinking about

c Guided oral exercises

i A dialogue between the boy and another person, who comes up and asks whether he can sit at the same table, then begins to chat with him.

ii A dialogue between two other people in the cafe, who know the boy and wonder why he is eating by himself.

iii A friend rings you up and tries to persuade you to go and eat with him. Make excuses for not going.

d Discussion

Do you often eat out? At midday or in the evening? Do you (ever) eat by yourself? What do you do on these occasions? (Do you read? Look out of the window?) Do you mind eating by yourself? Compare this picture with picture 19. What are the main differences?

Where can you get a good quick meal in your (town)? What sort of things can you have and how much would it cost to eat there?

54

a **Useful language**

factory area, backstreets
(coal) mine, pit head
late for work
dash down the street [round the corner]

b **Guidelines**
- who the boy is
- where he has come from
- why he is in a hurry
  (looking for someone/late for work/ ...)
- what happens after this

c **Guided oral exercises**

　i A dialogue between the boy and a friend, to whom he explains why he was late for work that morning.

　ii As you run round a corner, you nearly knock someone over. Apologise and explain why you are in a hurry.

　iii You are looking for a friend, who has hurried down the street ahead of you. Describe your friend to someone you meet, asking if he has seen him.

d **Discussion**

Imagine life in a town like this. Do you think the people who live here are well off? Why are the shops empty? Where do you think teenagers spend their free time?

This boy probably works down a coal mine. Are there mines in your country? (What for?) Find out what you can about conditions of work down a mine. How much have working conditions been improved over the last fifty years?

Imagine that you are able to plan a new town. What factors would you pay most attention to? Take into account in particular the question of housing, schools, shopping and recreational facilities. Where would you site the industrial area?

Describe any new town which you have visited or know of.

55

a **Useful language**

(a pile of) washing-up [dirty cups and saucers]
supper [breakfast] things
too tired to (do the washing-up)
feel fed up [worn out, a bit down]

b **Guidelines**
- who the woman is
- what time of day it is
- why she has a lot of washing-up to do
- why she has not done it
- how she feels
- whether she eventually does the washing-up

c **Guided oral exercises**

i A dialogue between the woman and (her daughter), who comes into the room and wants to know what the matter is.
ii You have a lot of washing-up to do. Try to persuade someone to help you.
iii You ring up a friend and find that he is very depressed. Find out what the matter is and try to cheer him up.

d **Discussion**

What would you do in this situation? Would you get on with the work? Do you have to help with the washing-up at home? Do you like (mind) it?

In many countries women want to be more free. e.g. they do not want just to become housewives. What is the attitude towards women's lib. in your country? Are women trying to be more independent? What do the men feel about it?

Give examples of some of the things that depress *you*. In every country there are certain problems in daily life (e.g. traffic, rising prices, shortages, pollution). Make a list of the ones which are prominent in your country and say which ones especially affect you.

56

a **Useful language**

(park) bench
have a rest [nap]

b **Guidelines**

- who these young people are
- where they are
- what they have been doing
- whether they know each other
- what the girl is thinking about
- what happens after this

c **Guided oral exercises**

i A dialogue between the girl and the boy, who wakes up and is surprised to find there someone he knows.
ii A dialogue between the boy and the girl, talking to one another for the first time.
iii You want to sit down on a park bench but the only available place is taken up by someone's (shopping). The person seems to be asleep. Ask the person to remove the things, apologising at the same time for disturbing him.

d **Discussion**

Do you ever go to sit in the park? What sort of people do you find there? Is it interesting to watch them?

Are there parks in the (city) where you live? Are they well looked after? Do many people go there?

Compare this picture with picture 28.

57

This is an 'association' game. Each student in the class or group (if the class has been sub-divided) is first asked to decide what connection there is between any two of these people.

Thus, for example, he may decide that, with reference to pictures 11 and 4, the old woman is the young girl's grandmother; that 10 is 5's teacher or employer; that 8 and 6 work in the same office or simply that 2 and 5 are friends.

Students are then called upon in turn to state their choice (e.g. *'I have chosen the woman in 1 and the man in 9')* and to say what connection they see between them (*'I think that they are married'* or *'She is the man's wife'*).

After this the student must be prepared to answer questions which the other students may ask him about the relationship which he has suggested. In this case the questions might be: *Who are they? Where do they live? How long have they been married? How old are they? Have they any children? (How old are they?) What's his job? How much does he earn? Does his wife have a job too? Is she a good cook? Are they happy?* etc.

In this way a picture of the relationship will emerge, and an oral summary might be given at the end by another student (students might take it in turns to keep notes and act as reporters). Other students may be asked if they chose the same pair and if so, whether they chose the same relationship. After this another student is called upon to state his choice and so the game continues.

Notice that many relationships can be set in the past, thus practising the Simple Past and related tenses as well as the auxiliary *used to* (e.g. *'9 and 10 were friends when they were young'* or *'12 used to work in 3's office.'*)

The game may also be played in teams. Thus the class is divided into two teams A and B. A student from Team A is called upon to state his choice. Students from Team B then ask him an agreed number of questions (say, five). If the student from Team A answers them satisfactorily, he scores a point for his team. A student from Team B is then called upon to state his choice and so the game continues.

At an intermediate level a handicap may be placed on each student after the first by requiring him to include one of the pictures already used by a previous student, so that all the pictures are gradually eliminated.

At an advanced level students may be challenged to improvise relationships between any two pictures.

58

This is also an 'association' game, which may be played in groups or with the class as a whole.

The students are asked to pair off each vehicle in the upper picture with one of the characters depicted below.

The teacher, or one of the students, then begins by asking: *'Who does the (motor-bike) belong to?* or *'Who owns the (old car)?'*

Students then take it in turns to state, and justify, their choice, which may be either an obvious one, such as *'The motor bike belongs to the young man in the leather jacket'* or a surprising one, such as *'It belongs to the man with the cigar.'*

In justifying his choice the student may be asked questions about the character under discussion or, at a more advanced level, asked to sketch in a background. E.g. *'The old car belongs to the man (in the fourth picture). He's a bank manager but his real interest in life is old cars. He doesn't drive the old car to the bank. He has a newer one. But he spends his weekends looking after the old car.'* etc.

59

Begin by making sure that the students can identify the 'profession' represented in each picture: e.g. lawyer, pilot, athlete, teacher, businessman, artist, doctor. These should be given in the most general terms to start off with. Later on it may be necessary to specify the activity of each more precisely. E.g. The doctor may be a general practitioner, physician, surgeon, specialist and so on.

The game may then be played in two ways. In the first variation (which is likely to appeal especially to the adolescent learner) students are asked to say what they are going to be or what they would like to be, when they grow up. Point out that they are allowed a 'free choice' if they like, as indicated by the blank square. Adult learners may be asked what they wanted to be or would have liked to be.

In the course of their discussions students should be encouraged to look at each profession critically, so that they can say why they would rather be (a pilot) than (an artist), or why they would not like to be (a teacher). At the end of the discussion, students may be asked to say whether they have changed their minds!

In the second variation students may be asked to speculate about each character depicted. For example, 5 looks like a man who works in an office of some kind. Is he a bank-manager, or a stockbroker, or ....? Why did he choose that profession? Does he enjoy it? Would he rather be a (teacher)?

This is perhaps best carried out as a group activity. The class may then be reassembled and each group asked to present a sketch of each character in turn, for comparison. In this way the preparation is done by the group, but each student may have an opportunity to talk about one of the characters.

60

This game is best played with the class divided into groups but may be played with the class as a whole.

Each student is asked to imagine that he will have to spend some time on a 'desert island', where, it is assumed, there will be vegetation, wild life and water. For his stay there he is allowed to take with him any three of the objects depicted — which will either be useful to him or help him pass the time. It may be advisable to name these objects before the game is played. The student may, if he prefers, have a 'free choice', as indicated by the blank square.

After the students have had sufficient time to make up their minds *which* objects they would take and *why* they would take them, one of them is invited to state his three choices. Notice that this can be done at an elementary level by saying: *'I'm going to take a (knife, a rope and some books).'* or at a more advanced level using: *'I would (like to) take (an axe, a mirror and a clock).'* The other students then ask him to justify each choice in turn, comment on it, argue with him and perhaps make counter-suggestions e.g. *'It would be better to take an axe rather than a knife, wouldn't it?'* Other students who have chosen the same object should be encouraged to 'defend' the student who is speaking.

When the pro's and con's have been adequately discussed, another student is called upon to state his choices.

The game may be repeated at a later stage by getting the students to state what they would *not* take.

61

In this game the students are asked to imagine that they have won a large sum of money. They are then invited to say how they are going to (or would) spend it.

The visual cues are not intended to be exhaustive but they should be found sufficient to stimulate a discussion at class or group level.

The students may discuss, for example, the advantages of buying a house compared with, say, the pleasures to be derived from having an aeroplane. They may be asked to decide between one 'pleasurable' possession and another (e.g. car, boat, aeroplane), and to weigh the advantage of one against another.

They may be invited to reject all these frivolous ways of spending money and to propose more useful alternatives such as founding a hospital or a home for children. They should be invited to consider the implications of suddenly getting a lot of money: e.g. the effect it has on people's lives. There are usually stories to be found in newspapers and magazines about what has happened to people, for example, who have won the football pools.

Where the students are working in groups, each group may be asked to make out a case in favour of spending the money in one particular way and then, through a spokesman, present this to the class as a whole. The various proposals can then be debated.

62

This set of pictures may be used to play a number of games. Once again it may be advisable to name all the objects before the game is played.

First, an association game may be played. For this each student is assigned, or chooses, one object and asked to decide what sort of person he associates with it. His description should be as complete as possible (within the limits of five or six sentences) and preferably written down (though perhaps in note form only) so that students are not tempted to make any changes when they compare their ideas.

Alternatively, they may be asked to link any three of these objects (e.g. the stick, the bag and the hat) and invited to explain how they fit into the way of life of the person they have imagined. For example, a student may decide that these three objects belong to a man who works in an office (What sort of office? What does he carry in his bag?). He often wears a hat (When? Why?), but he does not usually take the walking-stick with him (Why has he got one, then? Does he use it when he goes for walks at weekends? Did he get it when he was ill? etc).

A third possibility is to play a controlled guessing game, preferably in teams. A student in Team A, for example, thinks of one of the objects (and writes the name down on a piece of paper). Members of Team B are then allowed to ask, say, five questions in order to identify the object which the student has in mind. These questions should be of the kind than can be answered with *yes* or *no*: e.g. *Is it long? Can you wear it? Do you carry it? Is it made of metal? Is it expensive?* After this, Team B is allowed to guess the object. If they guess right, they gain a point; if they are wrong, a point is given to Team A, and so the game continues.

63/64

This is an 'alibi' game. It may be played in two ways but in either case this is best carried out as a group activity.

In the first variation, if the class is divided into four groups, say, two may serve as 'cops' and two as 'robbers'. The 'cops' are asked to think about the questions which they will ask. They may prepare these collectively or individually. The 'robbers' are asked to prepare alibis to prove that they could not have been involved in the robbery depicted in picture 63. For this purpose they may choose one of the situations depicted in picture 64 or invent ones of their own. After this, the groups pair off and the 'cops' question the 'robbers' one by one, trying to break down their alibis. Finally they decide which of the 'robbers' presented the weakest alibi.

Alternatively, two members of each group are asked to act as 'robbers'. They sit apart from the rest of the group, who will serve as 'cops', and prepare a joint alibi. They are then called across separately for questioning, the purpose of which is to make the second 'robber' contradict the first over small points of detail. The alibis are then compared by the group, who decide whether or not the two are guilty.

Note This game is described in detail in *Alibi* by B. Woolrich in English Language Teaching Vol. XVII No 3.

65

As the main picture shows, an office safe has been broken open. What kind of office it is, when the robbery took place and what was stolen may be left to the class or group to decide. Among the people who are working in the office the following are 'suspects', as shown in the smaller pictures: the office manager, the cleaner, the accountant or cashier, the porter, the secretary and the typist. Again appropriate background for each may be invented.

The main way of playing the game is as follows. Each student (or group, if the game is being played on a group basis) is asked to decide which of the suspects he thinks is guilty and to invent a little story why that person committed the robbery. For example, perhaps it was the accountant, who had been making false entries in the books and wanted to destroy the evidence. Or perhaps the manager himself was in league with a gang of criminals. The complete story is then built up through question and answer. If the game is played on a group basis, the students may work together to elaborate a complete story around one of the suspects, which is then reported to the other groups when the class re-assembles. Finally it can be decided which student or group produced the best story.

Alternatively, the pictures can be used to play an 'alibi' game (as with pictures 63/64). In this case students are assigned roles, asked to invent an alibi, and are then questioned by other students from the group or class serving as detectives.

66

Tell the students that each person depicted is being told or has just been told something over the phone and that they must try to imagine what was said from the expression on the faces.

Then either assign pictures to different students or let them choose their own.

After this they take it in turns to give their ideas, which are then discussed by the class or group.

Where two students have chosen or been assigned the same picture, their respective interpretations can be compared.

67

In this game the students are asked to decide which of the six persons depicted wrote the letter which the man is reading. Suggest one or two ideas to the class first (for example, if the first man wrote the letter, perhaps he is his bank manager or business partner; or, if the young girl wrote it, perhaps she is his girl-friend who does not want to see him again) and then ask them each to make up a story which will explain why the man is upset by the letter. As usual this can be followed up by discussion in the form of questions and comments by the other students.

68

This game is played by the students in pairs or divided into groups.

Explain to the students that they must link *any* one of the persons on the left with *any* one of those on the right and suggest what they are talking about. For example, the young man (top left) may be talking (taking the pictures on the right in order for purposes of illustration) to his father (headmaster, boss), to his brother (friend), to his grandmother or to his girl-friend (sister).

They may be asked either to outline what they are talking about (e.g. the young man is explaining to his girl-friend why he cannot see her that evening) and elaborate a little story around it, or to invent a dialogue around the situation. The latter exercise is a good activity when the students are working in pairs.

The stories or dialogues are later heard and discussed by the class.

To make the game more challenging, particularly at an advanced level, the pictures may be numbered and linked arbitrarily.

69

Before starting this game the students should be given a little time to make up their minds who owns which object, and what they think there is in each one.

The teacher, or a student, then starts by saying: *'Who does the (suitcase) belong to?'* or *'Who owns the (handbag)?'* A student is then called upon to answer. He may say, for example, *'I think it belongs to the young man on the right.'* He has then to explain why he thinks this: e.g. *'He's just going to university'* or *'He's just come back from holiday.'*

After giving more details, he is then asked to say what he thinks is in the suitcase. Other students may argue with him about his choice, giving their own opinion as to who owns the object and what is in it.

Students may be encouraged to assign the objects in an unexpected way. For example, they may give the shopping-basket to the old man. They must, however, be able to explain why he has it: e.g. *'His wife is ill, so he has gone shopping'* or *'He lives by himself and does all his own shopping.'*

For maximum practice the game is best played in groups.

70

a Language items

control [hold back, keep back] the crowd
wait to see sb. go by [pass]
catch sight [a glimpse] of
excited [eager, expectant, curious]

b Guidelines

— who or what these people are waiting to see
   (a famous person/a procession/ . . .)
— how long they have been waiting
— whether the police have a difficult job and if so, why
— what happens when the (person) passes
   (the crowd shouts/cheers/ . . .)

c Guided oral exercises

i A dialogue between two people in the crowd, one of whom wants to leave while the other tries to persuade (him) to stay.
ii You are one of the crowd but you cannot see what is happening because the person in front of you is very large. Ask him if you can change places with him.
iii Report to a friend your experiences the day you waited in a crowd for a famous person to pass by.

d Discussion

Have you been present on an occasion like the one shown in the picture? Tell us about it. If you see a crowd gathered, do you generally join them? How do crowds in your country behave on occasions like this? How do the police control them?

Who was the last famous person to visit your country (or city)? What happened that day? Give a brief report of the event.